Community Helpers

Construction Workers

by Tami Deedrick

Content Consultant:
Cheryl Harris
Executive Director
American Institute of Constructors;
Constructor Certification Commission

Bridgestone Books

an imprint of Capstone Press

Bridgestone Books are published by Capstone Press
818 North Willow Street, Mankato, Minnesota 56001
http://www.capstone-press.com

Library of Congress Cataloging-in-Publication Data
Deedrick, Tami.
    Construction workers/by Tami Deedrick.
        p. cm.--(Community helpers)
    Includes bibliographical references and index.
    Summary: An introduction to construction workers that examines their tasks, clothing, tools, and education.
    ISBN 1-56065-729-4
    1. Building--Juvenile literature. 2. Construction workers--Juvenile literature.
[1. Construction workers. 2. Building. 3. Occupations.] I. Title. II. Series: Community helpers (Mankato, Minn.)
TH149.D44   1998
624--dc21

                                                    97-35602
                                                      CIP
                                                       AC

Editorial credits
Editor, Matt Doeden; cover design and illustrations, Timothy Halldin;
photo research, Michelle L. Norstad

Photo credits
Betty Crowell, 10
Richard Hamilton Smith, 4
Unicorn Stock Photos/Eric R. Berndt, cover, 8, 16; Aneal Vohra, 6; Mike Morris, 12;
  Pam Power, 14; Dick Young, 18; Robin Rudd, 20

Table of Contents

Construction Workers

Construction workers are people who build things. They build homes, schools, and other buildings. They also build roads and bridges.

What Construction Workers Do

Construction workers have many jobs. They pour foundations. A foundation is the bottom of a building. Construction workers build walls on foundations. They also put roofs on buildings.

What Construction Workers Wear

Construction workers wear hard hats. The hats keep their heads safe from falling objects. Construction workers wear gloves to guard their hands. They also wear heavy boots. Many construction workers wear tool belts that hold their tools.

What Construction Workers Drive

Construction workers drive bulldozers to move dirt. They use cranes to lift supplies to high places. They drive trucks to carry concrete. Concrete is a mix that becomes hard as it dries. Construction workers use concrete to build foundations.

Tools Construction Workers Use

Construction workers use ladders to reach high places. They cut wood with saws. They use nails to hold things in place. They use hammers to pound nails. Construction workers also use levels. A level shows if a wall or floor is flat.

Construction Workers and Training

Some construction workers take classes.
They learn new skills. They also learn
how to stay safe at work. Other
construction workers learn skills as
they work.

Where Construction Workers Work

Construction workers work at construction sites. A construction site is any place where something is being built. Construction workers finish a job at one construction site. Then they move to a different construction site.

People Who Help Construction Workers

Architects help construction workers. Architects draw plans that show how buildings should look. Inspectors help by checking if buildings are safe. Engineers help by drawing plans for roads and bridges.

How Construction Workers Help Others

Construction workers help communities. A community is a group of people living in one area. Construction workers help by making safe homes and buildings. They also help by building safe roads and bridges.

Hands On: Stick Building

Construction workers use long boards called lumber to build things. You can build with craft sticks. Craft sticks come with frozen pops or ice-cream treats. Hobby stores also sell craft sticks.

What You Need
50 or more craft sticks   Glue
A table

What You Do
1. Lay two craft sticks side by side on the table. Move them three inches (eight centimeters) apart. Take two more sticks and glue them across the first two sticks. The four sticks should form a square.

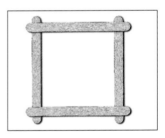

2. Build more squares. Glue the squares on top of each other. Try stacking 10 squares.

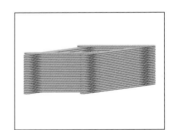

3. Give your building a roof. Glue sticks across the top of your building.

Words to Know

architect (AR-ki-tekt)—a person who draws plans that show how buildings should look
community (kuh-MYOO-nuh-tee)—a group of people living in one area
concrete (KON-kreet)—a mix that becomes hard as it dries
construction site (kuhn-STRUHK-shuhn SITE)—any place where something is being built
foundation (foun-DAY-shuhn)—the bottom of a building
level (LEV-uhl)—a tool that shows if a wall or floor is flat

Read More

Butterfield, Moira. *Bulldozers*. New York: Dorling Kindersley, 1995.

Hoban, Tana. *Construction Zone*. New York: Greenwillow Books, 1997.

Schomp, Virginia. *If You Were a Construction Worker*. New York : Benchmark Books, 1998.

Internet Sites

Build a Model Plank Road
http://www.sos.state.mi.us/history/museum/kidstuff/settling/build.html
Malcolm's Construction Trucks
http://www.malcolmdesigns.com/construction.html

Index